MANIFESTATION PATHWAYS

MANIFESTATION PATHWAYS

Letting Your Good Be There...
When You Get There!

RICHARD DOTTS

© Richard Dotts 2015

1st Edition

ISBN-13: 9781522875031

ISBN-10: 1522875034

Questions / comments? The author can be contacted at
RichardDotts@gmail.com

TABLE OF CONTENTS

CHAPTER ONE

THERE ARE NO ACCIDENTS
IN THIS UNIVERSE!

I was involved in a minor car accident a few weeks ago. The driver behind me misjudged their steering angle while changing out of our lane, and scraped my rear bumper. While no one was hurt, I could not help but think about whether I could have avoided the inconvenience in some way.

I started coming up with various possibilities. "Perhaps if I hadn't braked to let that bus in, the accident could have been averted. Perhaps if I had left the store earlier, that car wouldn't have been behind mine on the freeway. Or perhaps if I hadn't stopped for a drink on my way back, we wouldn't have met on the road…"

And so, endless possibilities and permutations about how the situation *could* have been different that day ran through my mind. "Perhaps if I had invited a friend to come along with me, I would have taken her home first and not taken my usual route…"

As I considered each of those possibilities, I had a sudden "A-ha!" moment. I realized that there was an infinite number of seemingly insignificant factors that could have been changed to avert the accident. For example, whether I stopped to pick up a particular item on the shelf that day would have affected the time I left the store, and hence where I was on the road at the time of the accident. Even the checkout line I chose that day could have played a part, for the speed of the store clerk determined the time I would have left the store! Yet all of these are only the conscious and unconscious decisions made on *my* part. One also has to consider the decisions made by the other driver and all others who interacted with us that day.

When you view the events in your life in this manner, you start to realize how mind-boggling the logistics behind a single manifestation can be. Even an event as simple as the chance encounter of two individuals has to be precipitated by millions of earlier events, in exactly the right sequence. These events involve not only the two main players, but also require the cooperation of all the other players in their world. If any of these preceding events had turned out differently, the course of the following events and hence the eventual outcome would be different. If I had stopped to admire the packaging on a can of dog food for just a few seconds longer that day, those few seconds would have given me sufficient leeway to avoid the accident. But what if the dog food manufacturer had chosen not to design an attractive and fun packaging for their product?

What if the store had chosen not to display it on that shelf, just in time to catch my eye? You get the idea.

There is an infinite number of splitting-off points which could have easily launched me into a different reality. But I was not drawn to take any of those alternative paths. Alas, I was at the perfect place at the perfect time. I was just where I needed to be, even if it eventually turned out to be an undesired manifestation.

The more I thought about it, the more I realized that there are simply no accidents in the Universe. There was no way I could have avoided the undesired manifestation because the hard truth is that I was there at exactly that time. I had made unconscious choices along the way that led me to that precise manifestation point, as did the other driver.

Try this simple thought experiment now, with an event from your own life. The beauty of this thought experiment is that you can do it with absolutely *any* event in your life—big or small, significant or insignificant. Of course, I recommend that you pick a fairly pleasant event in your life to look at. Once you have identified an event (for example, how you ran into a long lost friend at the shopping mall), try to recall the specific details of your encounter. You will soon realize that an infinite number of conditions had to be met in order for both of you to meet that day. You had to wander into a particular store or the right aisle at the right time, and so did your friend. Therefore, there is no way both of you could *not* have met under those circumstances. Everything was already orchestrated by the Universe and the manifestation was inevitable.

Many spiritual students have trouble understanding the concept of how there can be no accidents in our Universe. We tend to accept this saying when good things happen to us, but it can be difficult to do so in light of an undesirable happening. Many people have misunderstood this saying to mean, "You deserve the things that happen to you because there are no accidents. If you did not deserve it, it would not have happened." This is not what is meant by the saying at all. Deservingness plays no part here. Did I deserve to be in the car accident? Certainly not; I would not have wished it upon myself. Does someone deserve illness or any kind of negative suffering in their life? Absolutely not.

But the fact remains that I was indeed involved in the accident. I played a part in co-creating it. If I hadn't drawn that event to myself in some way, I would have avoided it very easily, simply by unconsciously taking a different route and jumping into an alternative reality at any one of the infinite splitting-off points. But I did not. I did the millions of things that led me to that precise manifestation moment. This is what is meant by the saying, "There are no accidents in life." It means that things do not just happen randomly to you. When something happens to you, it is always because you have attracted it to yourself in one way or another, often unconsciously. Many of our creations are unconscious, especially our undesired ones. However, the good news is that when you finally grasp these Universal principles, you have the power to turn your entire reality around and live life on your terms!

So how did I somehow "attract" that car accident to myself? Readers of my previous book, "Let the Universe Lead You", will know that I was led to my dream car in one afternoon following the reverse manifestation steps in that book. As I drove around in my new car, I found myself having worrying thoughts about what would happen if my beautiful new car was involved in an accident. True enough, the accident manifested itself just two weeks after I entertained those undesired thoughts for just a little bit. I have observed that manifestations happen extremely quickly for me now that I have cultivated a calm and clear inner state, which is why it is even more important not to engage in any undesired thoughts, especially if they relate to unwanted outcomes.

Abraham-Hicks explain this beautifully. They teach that everything in our lives is drawn to us either because we have wished for them at some point in time or we've thought about the subject. So yes, even thinking vividly about the things which you do not want activates similar vibrations within you, which can then go on to influence your outer reality if no contradictory intentions are held.

Instead of feeling fearful about bad things happening to you if you hold negative thoughts, see this as positive confirmation of these Universal Laws.

Know that the Universe works with mathematical precision and will give you absolutely anything which you place your focus upon, whether it is "good" or "bad" for you. The Universe does not discern between "desirable" or "undesirable" manifestations. It places no labels on your desires and will give you whatever you ask for. Therefore, nothing is off-limits or out-of-bounds for you. There is no such thing as a request that is "too big" to be fulfilled. Such labels are always self-imposed and can often become a stumbling block to our manifestations. Everyone is equally deserving of all the good there is in the eyes of the Universe.

When you realize this, you will understand why "bad" things can sometimes happen to "good" people and vice-versa. It is not because "good" guys finish last (another socially conditioned belief), but because these individuals have somehow allowed themselves to focus on undesirable outcomes. As I have shown above, this is often done unconsciously and without any second thought. When an undesirable outcome is held for long enough in one's inner state, with no contradictory intentions and without questioning, outer reality has to match up to that inner state. Similarly, "bad" guys who are strongly focused on their intent often get whatever "good" things that they ask for (even though they may be deemed "undeserving" by society), because the Universe treats everyone as equally deserving without judgment. All labels are merely self-imposed limitations.

This way of functioning may seem unfair at first. Why doesn't being good, gracious or kind in life make us immune to all the "bad" things that can happen to us? But look deeper and you'll realize a greater Universal Law at work here. There is no need for us to be "immune" from anything at all. Bad things *cannot* happen to you if you are not vibrationally compatible with them. This means that if you do not place any attention on unwanted outcomes or the undesirable aspects of your life, then you can live life experiencing only your highest good. No bad or evil can come to you, because you'll be so far apart from those negative experiences. It's as simple as that!

But so few people do it because they either have a misguided view of the Universe, or because they do not take the necessary effort to direct their focus and control their inner states. As you may have experienced, it can sometimes be difficult to withdraw our focus from the undesirable aspects of our lives. Instead, the natural human tendency is to keep talking about our problems and about what keeps us awake at night, in the hopes of finding solutions to our problems.

Know that the Universe has an infinite number of pathways to deliver your final end result to you. See this at work in your own life. Observe how the Universe has control over the billions of permutations of events to deliver your desired good to you in exactly the right sequence. Each the preceding events leading up to the final manifestation represents a splitting-off or turning point which can lead to an entirely new outcome. Therefore, just by changing one single variable in the whole scheme of events, a whole new reality can emerge. Figuring out which pathway to take at each splitting-off point is not your job. Lining up those events in exactly the right order is not your job. It is the job of the Universe.

Abraham-Hicks likens this to having a general manager at your beck and call. They have a wonderful analogy: imagine yourself as the CEO of a huge corporation with tens of thousands of employees, many of whom you have not personally met. Fortunately, you do not have to give instructions to each of the employees individually. Instead, you have the assistance of a capable general manager who organizes things on your behalf. All you have to do is to tell the manager what you would like and he executes your instructions by coordinating with the various departmental heads. Each time you set a new task for your general manager, he says, "Consider it done!"

Your life works in exactly the same way! You too, have a general manager of the Universe at your service, ready to help out in the fulfillment of your desires. All you need to do is to state your intentions clearly and consider it done! This general manager of the Universe (in the form of these Universal Laws) then coordinates all the events and logistics that are necessary for your final manifestation. Think of how exhausting it would be for the CEO to supervise each one of his employees personally. That's exactly what we try to do when we attempt to control the events in our lives and figure out how something is going to come to us, often unsuccessfully. Leave all of that planning and coordination to the Universe. Your job is to decide what you want and to focus on the final outcome wholeheartedly.

In line with our discussion, it is no accident that this book is now in your hands. Circumstances have made it such that *this* is the book you are now reading and not something else. I encourage you to read the pages that follow and implement the steps that resonate with you. Within these pages could lie answers to questions which you have asked in the past and will ask again in the future. At the same time, I encourage you to cherish all the current manifestations in your life, even the seemingly undesired ones. Those are often the manifestations that shine a light on our unconscious beliefs and behaviors. They point us to self-sabotaging patterns in our own life, which when dropped, can lead us to our greater good.

CHAPTER TWO

ONE SMALL SHIFT IS ALL YOU NEED...LET IT HAPPEN!

Before we begin our journey together, I would first like to set the stage by providing a broad overview of this work and how it relates to my previous books. The main focus of my previous books has been on cultivating an inner state that is conducive to our outer manifestations. I call this a manifestative inner state, in which any intention held on the inside against the backdrop of a calm inner state quickly becomes manifest in our outer reality. In turn, I shared tips and techniques for getting to a manifestative state, most of which revolved around the dropping of unwanted worries and fears.

Now that we have dropped much of our unwanted beliefs and programming, where do we go from here? How do we generate new possibilities for our future? This is where the current system comes in. I won't focus as much on the dropping of unwanted fears and worries in this book—although as always, a calm inner state is a prerequisite for outer manifestations. Instead, I will focus more on the aspects of becoming a deliberate and conscious creator. Now that you have freed yourself from the emotional baggage of the past, what would you like to create? You are no longer the unconscious creator from the past, not knowing why certain things happened to you. You now realize the powerful creative abilities that lie dormant within you. Armed with this knowledge, what would you like to create quickly and effortlessly?

This book is written to help you understand the mechanics of the creative process and how there are always infinite pathways to your good. Instead of figuring out which pathway is "right" for you (as many attempt to do with their logical mind), this book will explore tips and techniques that teach you to "feel" for your path of least resistance. The manifestation journey is one that is best taken with the heart and not with the mind. Similarly, this book is best read with the heart and not with the mind. Keep an open mind as you read, and let your heart (intuition) do the work. You already have all the answers deep within you. All you need to do is to follow the path, as pointed out by your higher self. Readers often comment about how my books awakened them to truths which they once lived but had forgotten along the way, affirming the reality that the answers you need are already within you. This is simply your natural way of being.

We start our journey by first knowing that there are infinite pathways to our desired good. As I explained in the previous chapter, the Universe has an endless number of ways to make anything happen for us. It can do so simply by changing a single variable in the whole scheme of events, which would drastically alter the course of future events. Having so many variables under its control means that you can easily engineer a small shift in your life right now that will lead to huge, transformational changes down the road.

Most people are under the mistaken impression that quantum shifts have to occur in their lives in order for their current situation to change. For example, if someone is in great financial debt, the tendency is to think that they need a windfall of a million dollars before their life can change for the better. This million dollars represents a self-imposed quantum leap that not only makes the person feel discouraged on the inside, but also sets up self-imposed limitations for him on the outside. In truth, the keys to the improvement of his financial situation may not be the quantum leap or miracle intervention that he so badly desires. Instead, it may be something as simple as stopping by a shelf and picking up a can of dog food.

Why is that so? The extra few seconds spent studying the packaging on that can of dog food may allow a chance encounter with an old friend, who may then introduce them to a new business associate. And that is merely <u>one</u> imagined possibility out of the millions of scenarios that the Universe can engineer. When you realize this, you'll understand why the Universe has a multitude of ways to make things happen for you.

The shift needed to resolve my mom's longstanding knee and back pain did not come in the form of a spontaneous, divine healing. Instead, it came in the form of an extremely small shift; that of meeting up with a friend who encouraged her to sign up at a ladies gym. Working out two times a week created a ripple effect that dramatically improved her emotional well-being and health. She is now able to not just walk, but sprint, up a flight of stairs, pain-free! If my mom had insisted that her healing come only in the form of specialist treatments or through health supplements, she would have unknowingly closed the doors to her own healing. Her body knew just what she needed to do to achieve optimal health. Let the Universe unfold its own path that is just right for your situation.

Whenever people tell me about their unfulfilled manifestations in life, the first thing I do is to look for ways in which they may be unconsciously "resisting" their manifestations. People often do so by insisting that their results come to them through a certain method or by believing that huge leaps and reality shifts are necessary to bring them their desired outcomes. Leave all of the small details to your general manager—to the Universe which knows better. My manifestations have come to me in various ways, through spontaneous shifts in reality and also through small events which I considered to be insignificant at the time.

For example, this series of books started with a single letter that was meant for a friend. I had no idea back then that a simple act of writing that long letter would transform my friend's life as well as my own. I had given that advice out of a genuine desire to help. I was acting from inspiration, and little did I know that it was the Universe's way of nudging me toward greater self-expression.

I can also recall instances in which I have unknowingly resisted my own manifestations. There was a time when I experienced severe pain in my left knee whenever I squatted. Due to the intensity of the pain, I assumed that it was caused by my intense, daily routine of cycling—which I had kept to for the past few years—and concluded that my knee cartilage was probably worn out. The thought made me extremely sad, as I had read that cartilages cannot be regenerated once worn out; another false belief I picked up from the Internet. I spent the next two weeks moving about in pain and unable to bend my left knee, all the while feeling extremely helpless and negative about the situation. It was not the pain, but the helplessness of the situation that consumed me.

One day, I felt inspired to drop by a pharmacy and take a look at a few supplements for my knees. I was pleasantly surprised to discover a transdermal form of glucosamine cream, along with an eye-catching diagram of the knee and a caption which read, "Rebuild cartilage!" in bright, bold letters. I felt a sense of relief wash over me as I read those words. I had previously believed that the situation was help-less, but those words pointed to an alternative real-ity. Reading those words gave me hope.

I bought the cream and three days after apply-ing it, my acute knee pain disappeared. I regained my previous range of motion as if the injury had never happened. Yet I know the pain I felt was very real. The most surprising observation was that I was able to stop using the cream and still the pain did not recur. Was it the cream that contributed to my spontaneous healing or was it something else?

Of course, I am not a qualified physician and this book is not meant to be a substitute for any medical advice. However, I now recognize that my refusal to believe in any alternatives back then led to the perpetuation of my old reality. I had errone-ously believed what I had read on the Internet and allowed myself to sink into a state of helplessness and depression. This was a self-imposed limitation caused by the closure of my mind to possible options or alternatives. I also know that the glucosamine cream did not heal me directly. Rather, it was my willingness to entertain an alternative reality that led to the final manifestation of healing.

The moment I opened my mind to the pos-sibility of healing and *focused on healing*, my body began to do whatever was necessary to return me to a state of perfect health. The longer I allowed myself to remain stuck on the unwanted aspects of my being (my pain), my body remained in that painful state.

The openness of your mind leads to an opening of sorts and a flourishing of options for you. We have already established that infinite possibilities exist at *any* time, no matter what the situation may be. It may be a case of acute knee pain or a case of "incurable" disease as diagnosed by doctors. But even in the most incurable of diseases, infinite pathways exist to health. The question is what are you going to focus on? Are you going to focus on the scary diagnosis itself given by the medical profession, or are you going to open yourself up to all the possibilities that exist out there? The Universe has an infinite number of ways to deliver your good to you.

A medical diagnosis is often difficult to ignore because we have been exposed to so many statistics and so much negative information that it scares the wits out of us. Even I was momentarily trapped by conventional "wisdom" by believing that my knee cartilages had degenerated and I had no way of healing that condition. I now recognize that it was my *fear* of the situation, rather than the situation itself that impeded my healing. The moment I found a way to take my mind off the fear itself and focus entirely on my desired outcome, the healing occurred very quickly.

It is the same for your outer manifestations. Are you focusing on the *lack* of options and the *lack* of what you have been asking for, or are you allowing yourself to be open to alternative outcomes and realities? Are you focusing on the one or two ways which you want things to happen for you, or are you open to *all* ways and *all* paths? One good affirmation to use is, "I will let my good be delivered to me in any way and any form possible." Feel this statement as you say it. Feel yourself opening up to the possibility of receiving your good in *any* form. I feel goosebumps all over my body and a sense of lightness just by repeating that affirmation to myself! Stop limiting your good by insisting that it has to be a quantum shift, or that it has to come through one particular channel! Accept any good that comes.

Just merely immersing yourself in the awareness that an infinite number of pathways exist will bring you immense benefits. That thought will energize and inspire you as you go about your daily activities. By going about your daily life steeped in this consciousness, you'll be signaling your intent to pick up on a wider range of nudges and signals from the Universe. So adopt a playful and carefree attitude here as you say and feel these words, "I don't care how my good comes to me. I don't care what form it takes. I don't care if my life shifts in a small or big way. I only know I recognize and act upon the impulses that the Universe sends me! I am open to everything, to all possibilities."

Walk around with this elevated level of consciousness and an appreciation for the infinite options that you have in each moment. Know that you always have unlimited options in every situation. You'll find miraculous things happening to you, simply by having this knowledge. Spontaneous manifestations, healings, improvements or subtle shifts will soon follow if you adopt this new mental attitude for the next week or so. Don't get ahead of yourself by figuring out what to do. That has never been your job. Instead, let the Universe lead you on the next step to take. For now, just rest in the assurance that nothing is off-limits, and that there are infinite ways in which your good can be delivered to you.

Chapter Three

The First Step to Manifestation

How is it possible that infinite options exist when all signs point to a dead end? This is where our limited physical perspective trips us up. When we attempt to analyze a situation from our current viewpoint, all we are able to access are past solutions to similar problems or possible solutions gleaned from various sources. But how many solutions can one humanly come up with in any situation? Probably fifty to one hundred if one thinks hard enough and is "creative." This figure still pales in comparison to the infinite pathways through which the Universe can make something happen for us. This is why figuring out the way to something has never been our job unless we feel inspired to do so. When we attempt to do something that we are not well-equipped to do, we end up with less than desirable results and a lot of negative feelings.

Looking back at my own life, I have observed that I am often wrong about how things will turn out. I may expect things to happen in a certain way, but reality always unfolds in a way that surprises me. I find myself reaching my desired goals with greater ease and flow whenever I concede control to the Universe and stop insisting on a particular way. Miracles happen when I willingly embrace all paths that are shown to me.

The greatest value in *any* situation is your ability to tune out all of the physical evidence and concentrate solely on the outcomes that you want. This ability is more important than most people realize. The sooner you are able to do so in any situation, the faster your manifestations will happen for you. Of course, the reverse is also true. I have seen manifestations delayed and held up for years, simply because individuals could not let go of their fervent need to repeatedly talk about (and focus on) their problems. You may think that rehashing a particular problem over and over again in your mind gives you a better chance of logically finding a good solution, but that assumption is what keeps people stuck in the first place. As I have explained above, the solutions we can humanly come up with given our best efforts still pale in comparison to what the Universe can do for us in an instant!

It does not matter what you are trying to manifest in your life. You may be trying to manifest a healthy body (a healing), more money, or a particular physical object. These principles work just as well for tangible or intangible manifestations. Anytime you place your focus on the *lack* of what you're asking for, your negative feelings of fear and discouragement let you know that you are focusing on the wrong aspects of the situation. This is why Abraham-Hicks emphasize the use of the emotional scale in letting us know whether we are focused correctly in each moment. Our negative emotions let us know that we are not only focused on an unwanted outcome but that we're also in the process of *creating* that unwanted outcome by virtue of our thoughts and feelings!

It can often be difficult to identify and focus on a desired outcome in the midst of a problematic situation. The most common scenario where this occurs is during a physical illness, in which the acute physical symptoms constantly remind an individual about their current undesired reality. For example, an individual may be in constant pain or may suffer from a restricted range of motion. Or there may be other symptoms that constantly remind them about the illness. It is under these conditions that focusing on an alternative, more desired reality will become particularly difficult. But it is *even more important* that one finds a way to do so under such circumstances, otherwise it will be difficult for healing to occur.

I experienced this firsthand during my two-week bout of knee pain. The fear of aggravating the pain was very much active within myself, so much that I was careful not to sit or squat in a particular way that would aggravate the pain. This is a classic example of how physical symptoms can impede the healing process. By being reminded of my pain for most of my waking hours, I was focused on an undesired reality most of the time, and hence unknowingly perpetuated more of that undesired reality!

It is a similar situation for individuals who find themselves in constant discomfort. Since the discomfort is with them around the clock, they find it difficult to focus on anything else other than the pain. One good remedy in these situations is to find ways to distract oneself from the pain, for example, by being engaged in an activity which one enjoys greatly. Watching funny videos can be a great distraction from physical discomfort. In other words, any activity that softens our focus on the undesired reality will be of great value. In accordance with these Universal Laws, people often find their physical situations improving once they reduce their focus on the undesired aspects of their reality.

What I have just brought up above is an example on one extreme end of the scale, in which a person is continually bombarded with reminders of their undesired reality and has no choice but to "face it." Fortunately, most of us are not in the same situation. We are not forced to confront an undesired physical reality with signs that are too big and too difficult to ignore.

The good news is that you actually have considerable leeway in most of life's situations. You actually have complete freedom in deciding what you want to place your focus on in each moment. Let's suppose that you are trying to manifest a fulfilling relationship. Of course, the absence of a lover can be particularly conspicuous if you keep focusing on the fact that you are alone, and that there is no one to accompany you to various activities. However, you can just as easily choose to exercise your ability to focus in other ways. For example, you can deliberately seek out and immerse yourself in solitary activities that do not require a partner. When you do so, you soften your focus on the current undesired reality (the lack of a partner) and shift into a more neutral state. Withdrawing your focus from an undesired reality is the first step to manifestations.

Some people have found success by acting "as if" something is already manifested. The reason why this works is because it cleverly redirects our focus from the current undesired reality toward our desired reality. For example, by acting as if your lover is already in your life and making the bed for both of you, you start placing your mental energy on the *presence* rather than the *absence* of a lover. This subtle difference in where you focus on the inside can make a huge difference to your manifested outcomes on the outside.

As you become more proficient at using your creative focusing abilities, you will realize that most problems in life are caused by scattered focus and misplaced thought energy. People often squander their thought energy by worrying about undesired outcomes, and then wonder why bad things keep happening to them over and over again. There are no accidents in this Universe! Whenever you continually rehash something on the inside with great feelings and emotion, it must come to pass!

A good example of this happened during my early days when I was trying to manifest more money for myself. Instead of placing my focus solely on the desired outcome of becoming financially wealthy, I instead chose to constantly worry about how little money there was in the bank. Although I was not living in poverty or debt, my thoughts constantly went back to how I did not have "enough money" in my bank account. Looking back, those beliefs were entirely self-created and self-perpetuated. Although creditors weren't knocking at my door, and I had enough money for my meals and living expenses, I still managed to create the false impression for myself that I did not have enough. Placing my mental focus on this false impression perpetuated my undesired reality, although I was not conscious of it at the time. It was only later on, after understanding these spiritual principles, that I saw how I was actually creating negative impressions all those years.

As you go about your daily activities, develop a heightened awareness of how you feel on the inside. Anytime you feel negative emotions or discomfort, immediately look within to identify the reason for feeling that way. I am not advocating that you dwell on the source of your negative feelings—rather, just become aware when negative feelings crop up for you. Those negative feelings indicate that you are focused on certain undesired aspects of your reality.

Let's suppose that you feel a sudden sense of worry as you are in the shower. Instead of brushing that feeling aside and suppressing it as most people tend to do, examine the feeling closely by focusing inwards. What are you feeling worried or fearful about? You'll find the answers coming to you if you are willing to ask. For example, your inner voice may say, "I am feeling worried about not having enough money to pay my bills." Aha! You have just uncovered a very valuable piece of the puzzle. Your worried feelings have just alerted you to the fact that you were focused on an undesired outcome (that of not having enough money to pay your bills). Had you allowed that negative feeling to continue, you would have been closer to manifesting that undesired outcome. Thus be thankful to your negative feelings for shining the light on how you are mis-creating in each moment!

Instead of dwelling on that worrisome outcome, immediately ask yourself this question, "What is it that I want in this situation?" In the beginning—and especially if one is prone to negative thinking—it can be difficult to quickly identify your desired outcomes. However, this becomes easier with frequent practice. Very soon, you'll be able to switch your focus and clearly state your desired outcomes, even in the midst of challenging situations.

Here are four examples of undesired situations and their corresponding desired outcomes. Note that different individuals may come up with different desired outcomes in each case. See if you notice a trend in each of these pairs:

(1) Undesired situation: "I am afraid I'll run out of money."

My desired outcome: "Peace about my finances."

(2) Undesired situation: "There is no cure for my condition and doctors can't find the cause of it."

My desired outcome: "Perfect health."

(3) Undesired situation: "I can't stand working with Mary. She makes my life difficult and makes me look bad in front of the bosses."

My desired outcome: "A harmonious working relationship and environment." (Notice how there is no need to specifically mention Mary in the desired outcome. This outcome means that everything and everyone, including Mary, will be well taken care of.)

(4) Undesired situation: "I can't stand driving my old car. It is always breaking down and needs expensive repairs."

My desired outcome: "Easily afford a new car."

In each case, the undesired situation describes the undesirable aspects of the current reality that you have allowed yourself to dwell on. You know you are focused on these unwanted aspects because of the negative feelings you feel on the inside. This is the purpose of our negative feelings, in that they let us know when we are in the process of creating our undesired outcomes.

Once you have been alerted to the fact that you are negatively focused, immediately identify a corresponding desired outcome and **state that outcome in as few words as possible**.

Did you notice a trend in each of the four pairs above? There is a tendency to use as many words as possible when describing our problems in life. That's why people are usually happy to elaborate upon and provide a lot of detail about their problems! However, in stating our desired outcomes, one should do the exact opposite. Be as **short and concise** as possible by representing your desired outcome in as few words as possible.

There is a reason for this. We are cultivating our ability to identify desired outcomes in the midst of challenging situations in life. Some of these situations may occur during chaotic or highly stressful times, where there is a tendency to be carried away by our own negative thinking. As mentioned, it is of great value in such situations to stop whatever we are doing or thinking and just affirm our highest desired outcomes for that situation.

I have found that it is difficult for me to come up with long sentences and affirmations in times like this. The solution is to do the exact opposite. Instead of trying to string up a long affirmation detailing how the issue *should* be resolved, affirm the highest outcome with a succinct sentence or phrase. You'll find it easier to come up with short sentences when using the process. A single sentence is all it takes to redirect your focus.

Try this the next time you find yourself complaining or going on and on about undesirable circumstances in your life: stop whatever you are doing and start looking for the desired outcome in that situation. It does not matter whether you think that outcome is believable and achievable, or otherwise. Remember that the Universe has infinite pathways to deliver your good to you. All you need to do is to identify what you want and state it. Then gently state your desired outcome in as few words as possible.

Notice how your focus automatically shifts the moment you do so. It always does! The moment you direct your mental focus toward another aspect of the issue (the solution and not the problem), you immediately start the process of manifesting that desired outcome. But as long as you are focused on complaining about how undesired or unjust the situation is, you'll keep attracting more of the same. Deliberately shifting your focus is the first step toward conscious manifestations in your life.

CHAPTER FOUR
THE SECRET PATHWAY OF LEAST RESISTANCE

No matter where you are in your life right now, and regardless of how the situation looks, always know that there are infinite pathways to your desired good. The majority of these pathways will remain invisible and unknown to you until it is time to traverse them. The right path will be shown to you by the Universe. It is important that you remind yourself of this spiritual truth as often as possible, as there is a tendency for individuals to be carried away by the "objective" physical evidence around them, so much so that they start believing in their own helplessness.

Spiritual masters know better than to believe in the physical world around them. They know that physical phenomena, no matter how real they seem, do not arise spontaneously by themselves. Rather, everything that exists in our outer world today is the result of a corresponding thought form that first existed in our spiritual (non-physical) inner worlds. This is also the reason why spiritual masters often refer to physical reality as an illusion. It is an illusion that is perpetuated by our inner worlds!

If we take a leaf from the book of these spiritual masters, then we'd know that the place to look when correcting any undesired situation in our lives is not on the outside. We do not try to influence physical people and events in order to correct undesired situations. That will just be tinkering with the effect but not the true cause. While it may *seem* to work for some time, the problems always recur in due course if the actual spiritual causes are not brought to light and dealt with.

We often see this playing out in real life. An individual who has trouble with their co-workers at their old company finds their new co-workers behaving in exactly the same way. A new lover repeats exactly the same behavioral patterns as the old one, and so on. Unless the true spiritual causes of a situation are dealt with, a person will keep attracting the same undesired situations in life by virtue of the same thought patterns that are repeated on the inside.

The cause of everything lies in our inner states. When we go right to the cause and work with the subtle energies at that level, everything in our physical reality straightens itself out. Therefore, if there is a delay in your physical manifestations, don't look to the physical world for your answers. The answers are not there, although they may *seem* to be. The physical world often gives us a lot of false information and confusing signals, thus compounding the initial issue. The true solution does not lie in taking a particular action or trying out a "secret" technique that has somehow been withheld from you. The solution, along with the answers to everything else, lie within you. If you are willing to look within for these answers, they will be shown to you.

When you understand this analogy of infinite pathways to your good, then physical manifestations become incredibly easy. All of the guesswork and figuring out what to do next to bring about the physical manifestation will be taken out of the equation. All of the uncertainty surrounding your manifestations will be gone.

Perhaps the most misunderstood part of manifestations is this: there is absolutely no need for you to figure out *how* something will come to you. That has never been your job. It is the job of the Universe to coordinate all the logistics involved and to bring you what you want in the most harmonious way possible. Only the Universe is aware of the infinite pathways through which your desired good can flow to you. Even your best efforts at identifying what these pathways are will be meager compared to what the Universe can do. As such, all you have to do is to become harmonious and aligned with these pathways, and allow themselves to unfold to you.

Before I realized this important principle, I was always tearing my hair out trying to "figure out" how I could make my manifestations happen for me. I was always preoccupied with methods and techniques that I could use to make them happen faster. I did not know that what I was doing was tinkering with the *how*, which was never my job in the first place. In fact, tinkering with the *how* only brought about more confusion and discouragement as I did not have a complete picture of what was happening. All of the resulting negative feelings only led to more delayed manifestations.

Nowadays, I adopt a very different view of manifestations; something I have been sharing in all my books. All I do now is identify what I want, before turning deep into my inner state and planting that intention there on the inside. That is all I have to do. I find that my desires usually manifest for me in a matter of days or weeks without my active intervention. Ever since I adopted this inner path to manifestations, I haven't had to worry about how something would come to me or how long it would take. Everything happened for me in perfect timing. I know deeply that even the desires which are not yet manifested in my life today will come true one day, and I never have to worry about the timing. Everything comes with divine timing.

In the beginning, it may not be easy for you to adopt this new way of living and thinking. However, I have developed a number of intuitive exercises which will make it easier in order for you to do so. I have tested these exercises in my own business and found them to work exceedingly well. I encourage you to try this new way of being for yourself over the next few weeks and compare the results to what you have achieved in the past. I think you'll agree with me that this new way which I'm about to share brings about superior results, even in the competitive corporate world.

By the time you identify what you want and clearly state your desired outcome, the Universe will have already identified all the possible pathways to your good. In fact, "identification" may not be the most appropriate word to use here since there is nothing to identify. There is an infinite number of pathways through which your good can come to you! Some of these pathways will involve a longer route than others, but they will all get you to the same outcome eventually.

At the same time, the Universe knows which ones are the shortest and most harmonious pathways to your good. These are the paths through which something you ask for will come into your life in the easiest ways possible. For example, you may hold an intention for something and receive it as a gift the next day. Or, you may hold an intention for something and be led to the exact place to buy it at the right price.

But why is it that our desires do not always come through these easier channels? One common reason is a simple lack of awareness about how our Universe works. When we are so caught up with figuring out how to achieve something, we often miss subtle cues from the Universe. We start acting from a state of necessity and fear, instead of inspiration, which is when we end up taking a longer route than necessary. Ironically, we move ourselves further away from our desired goals each time we try hard to make something happen!

I used to write up long to-do lists with tasks that I had to complete each day. Many of the tasks on my list were things I did not feel like doing, but I felt I had to complete them out of a sense of necessity or obligation. For example, I may not have felt like writing an article or making a phone call, but did so because I thought it would bring me closer to what I wanted. Sound familiar?

Corporate executives often experience this as an erosion of their own personal sense of freedom, where they find their inner purpose being taken over by external benchmarks and job requirements. I soon realized that it was a counter-productive way of living. More than half of the things I grudgingly engaged in did not bring me a sense of real joy. That was when I realized I had to change my way of operating in this world. I decided to live life on my terms in accordance with these Universal principles.

I did not ditch the to-do list entirely in the beginning. Instead, what I did was to adopt an intuitive way of living. I would scan the items on my to-do list and pick out the items that felt like the "path of least resistance" for me. Invariably, one or two items on the list always felt easier or simpler to do than the rest. I would do those ones first. I used my intuition (and not my logic) when going through the list. The tasks I picked were not always the easiest or simplest in terms of complexity or procedure, but they felt right for me to complete at that time. Something was nudging me to do them first. I was listening to my inner voice and letting it guide my outer actions, instead of the other way around.

The first week I tried this new way of working, I was hooked and I never went back. I completed tasks in one-third of the time doing only the things I enjoyed the most. I removed any task that remained on the list after several iterations, as those were the tasks that did not align with my highest self.

What I did not know back then was that I had unknowingly tapped into these powerful manifestation principles. I was letting the Universe show me the path of least resistance and acting from a sense of inspiration instead of fear. I have to add that I did not experience any negative consequences as a result of leaving certain tasks undone. When I didn't do the things I believe I "had" to do in order to advance my business, I was still led to great abundance through other means. All my previous fears were unfounded. We cannot be led to any harm when we follow our highest calling and live from a state of pure inspiration.

Try this to-do list exercise for yourself over the next few weeks or so. You can use a traditional pen-and-paper to-do list, although the technique works just as well without a physical list. All you need to do is to ask yourself what *feels* the most natural for you to do next, out of all the things that need to be done at a certain time. Then just go and do it! It's as simple as that. Use this process each time you finish a task and move on to the next. It works just as well in both your personal and professional lives.

At first glance, this may seem like a technique solely for increasing your personal productivity and effectiveness. However, this exercise cultivates a far more important skill that will lay the foundation for the rest of this book.

What you are actually doing is developing your ability to **intuitively identify the path of least resistance in any situation**. Each time you pick a task on your to-do list that feels right for you—you act from a state of inspiration and let the Universe point out the path of least resistance for you in that situation. In addition, the use of a to-do list creates a structure for this exercise and helps you to overcome any objections your logical mind may have about relying on your inner guidance. Thus, this exercise is a great way of blending both the conscious and intuitive aspects of your being. It helped me move away from my purely rational ways of thinking and acting in the world.

Miraculous things have happened as a result of applying this method, and we have not even discussed the specific applications yet! For example, I may suddenly feel an impulse to do something on my list which has been sitting there for the longest time, but without really knowing why. I have felt a sudden nudge to make a phone call, only to discover that I made the call at just the right moment to speak with the right person. Life becomes easy and effortless once you tap into this principle of infinite manifestation pathways and allow yourself to be led toward your path of least resistance in every moment.

Chapter Five

Feeling for the Path of Least Resistance

In the last chapter, I described an exercise that can strengthen your intuitive abilities to *feel* for the path of least resistance. Why is it so important to *feel* for this path, as opposed to using your logic to figure out which action you should take next?

The path of least resistance is always present in any situation. No matter where you are in life right now or how your current situation seems, there are always a few paths of least resistance which you can easily take. These paths represent the fastest and most direct routes to your desired outcome. In most cases, our logical, rational minds prevent us from taking these paths because of its limited perspective and unconscious limiting beliefs. For example, we may unconsciously hold the belief that "life is a struggle" or that "physical ailments take a long time to heal." These unconscious beliefs, as innocuous as they seem on the surface, prevent us from recognizing and following the steps that lead to our greatest good.

Many people wonder why they have such a difficult time manifesting more financial abundance in their lives. A closer look at their unconscious programming often reveals the following beliefs: "It is difficult to make money. Money is difficult to come by. My current circumstances do not allow me to increase my income. I have no time to explore other options." While these beliefs sound like innocent statements, they prevent an individual from recognizing their paths of least resistance even when these paths are laid out right in front of them!

In my earlier work as a consultant, I often met with entrepreneurs who lamented the lack of opportunities in their industry. They would often tell me how everything has been "done to death" in their field, and that there was a lack of "greener pastures" into which they could expand. However, as an outsider to their business, I was able to look at their field and come up with all sorts of profitable new possibilities. I was able to do so not because I was smarter or more experienced than them, but because I actually knew next to nothing about their industry! My fresh eyes allowed me to bypass the usual blind spots and limiting beliefs that tripped them up. Putting my ideas into action while guided by their expertise led to new possibilities, which in turn opened up more doors for their business. Thus the creative cycle perpetuates itself in business, led by entrepreneurs who are willing to explore new ways of doing things.

The same thing is happening in your life right now. You are so familiar with your current ways of operating in this world that everything seems to be cast in stone for you. You may have done things in the same way, and for the longest time, that you no longer question your actions or underlying assumptions. You just go through the motions each day. If you stopped to question your thinking even for just a single moment, you would be shocked at how much of what you currently do has no practical basis at all. You simply do it because that is the way that things have always been done in your family or in your community.

I am not advocating that we all become renegades this very moment and start acting out of line—what I recommend instead, is that you start a spiritual revolution *on the inside.* Adopt a completely new way of operating in this world based on these spiritual truths and a new way of life shall emerge for you. Not only does this new path take *less* effort than before, but you will also achieve your goals in a much shorter time, and with much less stress and emotional turmoil. Since applying these manifestation principles in my life, I have completely removed "stress" from the equation. I no longer feel stressed out by the circumstances in my life because I know that anytime I begin to feel stressed out, it is because I am getting ahead of myself by doing something which is not my work.

Your work is to identify what you want and then hold a mental picture of that outcome clearly in your mind. We covered how to do this in Chapter 3. After you have identified your desired outcome, you then start *feeling* for the path of least resistance in any situation. I gave you a taste of how this feels in the previous chapter, where you applied the process to your daily to-do list. Now that you have experienced the basics, let's apply them to your life and your actual manifestations.

If I had asked you to *feel* for the path of least resistance outright, many people would have rejected this method as it is not how we have been taught to function in life. Most people feel more comfortable *thinking about* what their path of least resistance should be as opposed to *feeling for it*. However, this way of living hasn't brought you happiness or everlasting success in all this time. If it had brought you some results, those results would have been accompanied by a lot of stress and emotional pressure. I know, because I have been through that way of living myself. A logical way of living where you try to figure everything out by yourself, wears you out—and is against the flow of the Universe.

Think back to the earlier to-do list exercise, which I hope is a mainstay in your life by now. The exercise is meant to illustrate a few important principles. You will realize—after trying the method for some time—that the action you feel inspired to take is not always the action that you think you should logically take. In other words, the paths you arrive at when you use your logical mind and your intuitive guidance are often different. Very rarely do they converge. Another way of saying this is that your heart and your head often give you different directions. If so, which one should you follow?

Spiritual teachers have often taught that when our head and hearts are in conflict, we should always go with our heart. I probably read this piece of advice about a thousand times and yet still found it difficult to put into action. After all, my head was giving me many good, sound and logical reasons to base my decision upon, while my heart could give me no good reasons, other than a mere "good feeling" on the inside!

And so for the first part of my life, I went with my head most of the time. As I became more aware of these spiritual principles, I realized that following our hearts is not a sign of irrationality or weakness but is actually a sign of wisdom. The heart knows what the head cannot even communicate in words and logic. The heart is Universal guidance trying to point us toward our greater good.

I can relate countless stories of how each time I overruled my heart and followed my head—I often had to work even harder to get myself out of some undesirable situation later on. I can also unequivocally state that following my heart has never put me in any harm or danger. When you follow your highest guidance, you will always be led toward your highest good.

This is why I strongly encourage you to try the to-do list exercise for yourself and discover the difference between *thinking* and *feeling* for the path of least resistance. Try to feel what your path of least resistance is, rather than trying to figure it out through logic. Adopt this new way of living for the next few weeks or so and compare the results. That is the only way which this head-versus-heart debate can be put to rest. It wasn't until I finally proved it to myself that I was convinced the Universe always knows what is best for me.

The greatest value of the to-do list exercise is that it shows you what an intuitive nudge feels like for you. As you go through each item on your to-do list, become aware of how you feel on the inside. Some items (paths) will feel different from the rest. For example, when I think about a task which I do not feel like doing, I immediately feel a tightness in my chest along with a sense of heaviness and inertia. That is my body's unique way of letting me know that I am not acting in accordance with my highest good. However, when I think about a task which I feel inspired to do, the feeling I get on the inside is completely different. That sense of tightness and constriction gives way to an easy, flowing sense of joy and lightness. I immediately feel myself becoming very much alive on the inside.

As you become more sensitive to how the Universe sends you intuitive nudges through your inner senses, you'll be able to identify when you should take a particular action and when you should not. The to-do list exercise gives you the opportunity to feel for these differences many times throughout the day. At the end of a month or two, you will have made thousands of comparisons and you'll become proficient at identifying your paths of least resistance through *feeling* alone. You will instinctively know which alternative feels right for you and which feels not-so-right.

When you have mastered the process of feeling for the path of least resistance, it is time to take the next step. The to-do list was an artificial construct we put in place to create some structure for the earlier exercise. But there is no to-do list in real life. Instead, think of a list containing an infinite number of pathways and items. Each item on that Universal list represents a new possibility. The good news is that you do not have to do all—or even most—of the items on the list. You do not have to take every single pathway. Just following a single path is needed for physical manifestations to occur in your life. The Universe will show you the appropriate steps to take at just the right moment.

To *feel* for the path of least resistance toward your manifestations, it helps to first settle into a calm and peaceful inner state. Close your eyes and focus on your breathing. I like to take three deep breaths before I turn inwards, inhaling fully and exhaling slowly while letting my physical body relax. I take as much time as necessary to get myself into a relaxed and peaceful inner state.

When you are completely at peace and relaxed, gently bring your desired outcome to mind. It helps to work with only one outcome or intention at a time. Some people bring this desired outcome to their mind by repeating the outcome statement identified earlier. For example, you may use "peace about my finances" as the statement to symbolize your desired end result about your finances.

There is no need to describe your desired outcome in overwhelming detail. When you do so, you are going into the details about the problem and imposing your own limitations on the situation. If you are in financial debt, it is more than sufficient to affirm "peace about my finances" and leave it at that. There is no need to say, "I intend to have a supplementary income of $5000 a month to pay off my debt and an additional $2000 for living expenses every month." That would be going into too much detail about the undesired situation that you want to get rid of. Furthermore, the Universe knows better than you do. The pathway to your intended outcome may *not* be the supplementary income which you have imagined. Resist the urge to state what you think would be the solution to your perceived problems.

Similarly, if you experience physical ailments in your body, it is sufficient to affirm "perfect health" and leave it at that. Use the words that feel right for you. There is no need to say, "I wish for the pain in my knee to be gone and my back to stop hurting. I intend for the new nutritional supplements to work for me." Do you see how by going into such great detail, you have dictated that your healing only comes through the pathway of consuming nutritional supplements? So don't limit yourself in this manner. Open yourself up to any and all possibilities. That is the most powerful way toward your physical manifestations.

Immediately after affirming your desired outcome statement, relax and *feel* for the pathways that present themselves to you. Again, the difference between figuring something out using your rational brain and feeling for a solution will be subtle at first. You may think a particular solution has just popped up intuitively for you, when in fact it may be something conjured up by your logical self. This is when the earlier cues from the to-do list exercise come in handy. If you pay close attention, you will feel the difference between a solution that is arrived at through logical reasoning and one that is presented to you from your higher self. Just gently let any logical or intellectual solution go.

Your intellectual mind may instinctively try to solve the problem the first few times you try this exercise. However, as you become more proficient at quieting the rational mind chatter, you will find intuitive solutions floating more freely up to your conscious awareness. These are the pathways of least resistance for you. The purpose of this inner exercise is not to actively come up with solutions or to make anything happen in your life. Rather, it is to allow the pathways of least resistance to present themselves more clearly to you out of the myriad of possibilities that exist.

Chapter Six

Letting the Path Unfold for You by Asking a Simple Question

In the past few years of my life, I have found great delight in letting the path unfold for me. I have found this to be a much more effective and joyous way of living than constantly trying to figure out the best path to take next. Lao Tzu explained this most beautifully when he wrote in the Tao Te Ching, "In the pursuit of learning, every day something is acquired. In the pursuit of the Tao, every day something is dropped. Less and less is done, until nonaction is achieved. When nothing is done, nothing is left undone."

Lao Tzu's "pursuit of the Tao" refers to the understanding and successful application of these Universal principles. The word *tao* means Universal Laws. What Lao Tzu has written above fits perfectly into the theme of this book. In fact, if you can fully understand and internalize Lao Tzu's words, then you will live in bliss for the rest of your life, without the need to use another manifestation "technique."

The western way of knowledge and learning emphasizes the use of logic and the acquisition of additional pieces of information to help guide our decisions. Western decision-making is all about collecting more data points. To the contrary, a mastery of these Universal principles entails the exact opposite. It is not about the acquisition of new methods or new knowledge, but rather about the dropping of our old, unresourceful and false beliefs about the world. Hence, spiritual mastery is about the *dropping* of negative beliefs, habits and thought patterns as opposed to learning new techniques to better our lives.

It is the same when manifesting our desired good in life. Manifestations are not about using new techniques and methods to "make something happen" on the outside. There is often a certain allure about the use of persuasive or even manipulative techniques to achieve what we want in life. The commercial market is not short of peddlers hoping to sell us ways and means of manipulating people to get what we want—ranging from hypnosis, to mind-control techniques, even to magical spells! I am often asked by some of my readers whether I have any magical techniques that will make their manifestations happen faster! They are so desperate to get what they want that they're willing to try anything.

While these persuasive or manipulative techniques may work in the short run, they ultimately fail for two main reasons. First, these techniques prevent us from realizing the true creative powers that are within us. They reinforce the need to use outer methods to control the outer world around us, which is an illusion unto itself. Second, these methods are not in accordance with Universal Laws. No one can ever be forced to do something that is against their will. Therefore, while you may coerce someone to act in a particular way in the short term, your ruse will always fall through in the long term, when the individual realizes their own innate freedom of choice.

Somewhat presciently, Lao Tzu ended his previous statement with, "The world is ruled by letting things take their course. It cannot be ruled by interfering." This sums up the core message of this book: the Universe knows the best ways through which your desired good can come to you. Let the Universe take its course and let the pathway of least resistance unfold to you. Your interference in how things unfold can only serve to delay your manifestations.

In my early days of studying Abraham-Hicks, they proposed the use of a leading question to let the path of least resistance unfold to me. Abraham-Hicks suggested that I ask the Universe, "Do you know what I want? Show me what I should do next!" I always found their suggestion absurd and preposterous, as if the Universe would answer me personally!

It was only in later years that I realized the immense power of this practice. In my early days, I was trying to use the above statement while feeling a lot of negative emotions, as if *demanding* the Universe show me what I should do next. I was demanding concrete proof of my manifestations from the Universe. Of course, asking the Universe under those circumstances yielded no answers, only more frustration. The Universe can only give us what is in harmony with our dominant feelings and intentions.

However, as I loosened up over the years and let my deep sense of worry go, I began asking the question above in a playful, childlike and detached manner. It's as if one is asking a lover somewhat flirtatiously, "Do you know what I want? Surprise me!" This is the carefree and delightful attitude which we are going for here. I have also found that you do not even have to physically ask this question in words. Some people may find it more effective to say the above sentence out loud (when you're alone, of course) throughout the day. Others may find that simply holding a sense of expectancy is all that is required.

Notice how you feel after asking the question above. If you have trouble saying it to the Universe, then imagine saying it to a lover or a loved one who cares deeply about you and wants you to be happy. Notice how it feels when you ask the lover somewhat playfully, "Do you know what I want? Surprise me!" This is the feeling of detachment and joy we are going for here. We expect good things to happen to us next and are therefore open to all possibilities, yet we are not worried about when or whether they will happen, as we trust our lover completely. Once you capture the emotional essence of this question, ask the same question to the Universe.

As you go about your day, pose this question to the Universe frequently: "Do you know what I want? Show me signs of what I want!" This question must be posed in a detached and playful manner. If you ask this question while immersed in the right inner state, then you'll find that the Universe reciprocates every single time with physical signs and clues that delight you. The path of least resistance in any situation then unfolds for you effortlessly.

When one has done everything they can to visualize and affirm their desired outcome, it is time to leave the physical unfolding to the Universe. The best way to do so is to go about your daily activities with a sense of detachment and expectancy. This can sometimes be difficult to do when we find ourselves overly attached to a particular outcome, or when the outcome is important to us. For example, it can often be difficult to manifest things and conditions which you *really* care about, while things which are not particularly important in your life seem to happen spontaneously and easily. The reason is because we are often so attached to the outcome of those important subjects that we end up interfering in the unfolding process.

Posing this playful question to the Universe shifts your focus from one of interference and insistence on a particular pathway to one of allowance. By asking this question, you give up control to the Universe and begin to *feel* for your path of least resistance, as opposed to *thinking* about it. The best-feeling path in any situation is your path of least resistance.

Manifestations can happen in as little as a few hours after you adopt the above mindset. But remember, the key here is to throw out the question above in a playful and detached inner state with absolutely no expectations of the outcome. If you are asking the question with the hope of soliciting a *sure* answer or a *sure* path from the Universe, then you are trying too hard. Your own negative feelings and vibrations about the issue will delay the manifestations even more. The Universe always picks up on the true essence of how you are feeling on the inside and amplifies those feelings for you.

Each time I asked the question above (either in the form of physical words or in the form of an expectant yet detached curious feeling), the answers have come to me extremely quickly. Readers of my book "Let the Universe Lead You" will know the story of how I was led to the purchase of my dream car in one afternoon. The physical signs came shortly after I asked this question of the Universe. But the use of this question is not limited to making specific manifestations happen in your life. You can also pose the question in a general sense, and notice how the Universe responds beautifully to you each time. When you are playful with the Universe, the Universe will be playful and supportive of your efforts. There is no way you can do any of this incorrectly, other than your own insistence that there has to be a "right" way.

Experiment with asking this question in different areas of your life. Ask the Universe (playfully, of course) to surprise you about your finances and then notice the myriad of ways through which it does. That is when you will often experience delightful things happening in relation to your financial circumstances. You can also do so in the areas of relationships, career and health. The applications are truly limitless, which is why this process is so powerful. But the key is that you have to ask with the right inner state and not from a place of worry or of lacking. Sometimes the physical signs happen the moment you ask, without the need for any active physical intervention on your part. For example, you may spontaneously come into contact with a sum of money. At other times, you may be nudged to take various paths that will eventually lead to your highest good. As I wrote in the opening of this book, there can be no accidents in life.

Most people find it somewhat disconcerting that even after asking for a long time, the path of least resistance is still not presented to them. This often happens when you try *too* hard and keep looking out for physical signs around you. Once again, trying *too hard* to achieve something is counterproductive when it comes to applying these Universal principles. These principles are about non-doing and non-action as opposed to actively *doing* something. There is no need to look out too hard for possible signs and clues for fear that you may miss something. When the Universe has something important for you to act upon, you *will* know it and the Universe will keep nudging you in the right direction until you know it.

Many people tell me that nothing is happening in their lives despite asking so hard for what they want. In every case, the reason is because the individual has still not learned how to let go of his need to figure out the solution for himself through active thought. Let go of your need to actively and logically think of a solution. Even the sharpest mind does not know all the possible pathways as completely as the Universe. Instead, what one should do in any situation is to jump straight to affirming (focusing on) the final outcome and leave it to the Universe to present the possible pathways. You'll find that the Universe does so more efficiently and effectively than your logical mind can.

As you go about your daily affairs, you may feel a sudden inclination or nudge to take a particular course of action. When this nudge happens, check within to see how it makes you feel. Do you feel a sense of dread and inertia, or is there a sense of lightness and joy surrounding this particular suggested action? A sense of underlying inertia usually suggests that the nudge is not from the Universe, but merely a pathway conjured up by your logical, reasoning mind. On the other hand, a sense of lightness and joy in which everything feels right for you points to higher Universal guidance. If you'll just follow that nudge and act on it, then nothing can go wrong for you.

The differences between the two are usually subtle, especially in the beginning. That's why the purpose of the to-do list exercise was to help you effectively discern between these two types of inner feelings quickly. You'll soon be able to tell when a pathway is one that has been conjured up by your logical mind, and when you are receiving inspiration from the divine. Once again, thinking and logic play no part in any of this. Always pay attention to your *feelings* and notice the differences in how you feel on the inside when you think about each pathway.

CHAPTER SEVEN

UNDERSTANDING ACTION VERSUS NON-ACTION PATHWAYS

Perhaps nothing is more misunderstood than the role of physical action in our manifestations. On one hand, there is a widespread belief that things will not happen if you do nothing once you've asked for what you want. On the other hand, the great spiritual masters (such as Lao Tzu from the previous chapter, and Abraham-Hicks) speak clearly of the overriding importance of non-action and non-interference in the affairs of the Universe, and how there is no need for us to do anything in order to get what we want.

I have realized that holding misguided views about the role of physical action in the creative process often trips us up and delays our physical manifestations. Having swung between both extremes in the past—depending on which stage I was in my life at that time—I now have a better understanding of the whole creative process. So let's lay a few of those misguided beliefs to rest.

The first and foremost question on everyone's mind will be this: is it possible to manifest something without taking *any* physical action at all? In other words, is it possible to merely hold an intention for something and then have it spontaneously come true for us, without a single bit of physical action on our part? Readers of my books will know that the answer is a resounding "Yes!", in that it is certainly possible to hold a pure intention for something and have it appear in our lives a few days, hours, or weeks later.

Manifestations can happen when we least expect them. I have experienced this kind of spontaneous manifestation for myself countless times, so my personal experience certainly validates the view espoused by the great spiritual teachers. One of my favorite examples of this kind of manifestation is receiving an unexpected check in the mail; something which I did not have to physically "work" for. Such checks in the mail are regular occurrences for me now. Another of my favorites is rescheduling or canceling an appointment without having to pick up the phone to inform the other party or discuss our availability. Instead, the other party reschedules the appointment to fit *my* schedule instead, without any active intervention on my part! Dr. David Hawkins writes of how his desired meal was brought to him at a restaurant, simply by holding a pure intention for what he wanted to eat and without having to physically order the meal from the waiter. Talk about a divine intervention! These occurrences are possible in our everyday lives once we are willing to broaden our beliefs about what is possible.

Now let's take a look at the other extreme: have I had manifestations come to me only after I took a particular physical action (or series of steps) to achieve them? Definitely, since there were also times in my life when I walked right into my desired good by being at a particular place at a particular time. I was inspired to take the right action at the right time, which led to the final manifestation.

Someone who does not understand the Laws of the Universe will think that I am contradicting myself or that the Universe is somewhat inconsistent. Why is it that no physical action is needed in the former case, while some physical action is needed in the latter?

Instead of seeing this as an inconsistency, view it as the different pathways through which your desired good can come to you. Our good always flows to us through the path of least resistance. In turn, our path of least resistance depends on a number of factors, most important is **our inner state at a particular point in time**. Therefore, depending on our level of expectancy and allowance, some of our desired good enters into our lives through shorter and more direct pathways, while some of our good may come through longer pathways.

The pathways through which our good can come to us is not within our control. But what we *can* control is how we feel about our manifestations on the inside, our inner states. This inner state is key in determining the speed and efficacy of our manifestations. One of the ways in which we inadvertently delay our physical manifestations is to worry about *how* or *when* they will come to us. Worrying about the *how* or whether something will happen puts us in a non-receptive state to receive our good, which ironically closes off the more direct and straightforward pathways. Instead of spontaneously walking right into your good, you may now have to take a few more detours to get them.

So what is the role of physical action in our manifestations? I would say that while physical action is present in almost all of our manifestations, deciding on the course of action to take has never been our job. Neither is taking a particular action solely for the sake of making something happen, unless one feels inspired to do so. This means that we never have to act against our will and we never have to do things that we don't feel like doing. You can be assured that these actions are absolutely unnecessary to the fulfillment of our desires. All too often, people beat themselves up by saying things like, "I don't feel like doing this, but in order to achieve that, I have to." That is a misconception about the role of physical action and how much it contributes to the eventual manifestation of your desires. The fact that you don't feel like taking a particular action means that it is *not* the path of least resistance for you. And while you can certainly force yourself to take it, that is not the shortest path that the Universe has planned for you.

This is the reason why the role of physical action in our manifestations is often grossly overstated. From our limited human perspectives, it seems perfectly logical to attribute a manifestation of something to the physical events that preceded it. But in doing so, we would be ignoring all the other parts of the equation and neglecting the power of our inner guidance and thoughts. Most people think it is their outer actions that led to their eventual manifestations, when in fact much credit should also be given to the inner nudges that spurred them to take those actions in the first place. Without those inner nudges, the manifestations would not have occurred.

Do yourself a favor today and leave all the hard work to the Universe. The hard work includes second-guessing which path you should take at any one time, and how you should behave in order to increase your chances of achieving your goals. The Universe already knows all of that, so **let it guide you and show you the way**. It can only show you the way if you are receptive to its guidance, not if you are always overriding your intuition with reason and logic. This is why it is so important to quiet the rational, thinking part of your mind and let the natural impulses well up from within. These impulses will point to the path of least resistance.

The path of least resistance differs in every situation because we are all at different stages in our lives. Our level of consciousness (our inner state) plays a significant role in dictating our path of least resistance as well. For example, if you do not yet believe that spontaneous healings are possible, then the path of least resistance for you may be to explore a natural health alternative—at least for the time being. Yet for someone who does not believe in anything other than conventional Western medicine, then the path of least resistance for that individual may lie within the realms of conventional medicine. Similarly, if you do not yet believe that spontaneous manifestations without physical action are possible, then the path of least resistance for you may be a path in which you have to take some action in order to guide things along.

Just reading a book like this has the power to elevate your level of consciousness. I use the word "elevate" not to suggest that these teachings are superior, but to refer to how these teachings make you ponder the alternative realities and pathways which lie beyond the realm of your expected, everyday reality. The more you are willing to entertain these alternative realities, the more you allow them to happen in your life. This is how your reality shifts. Merely by holding a possibility in mind and *knowing* that it is possible, you evoke an expansion of your current reality.

This is why manifestation is largely an *inner* process of creation, as opposed to an outer process of controlling external circumstances and events. There is only so much physical effort we can take.

Oftentimes, even working ourselves to the point of exhaustion accomplishes much less than what we can achieve through focused mental effort. This is why manifestations are about doing the inner work—deciding what you want, holding that outcome in your mind and then *feeling for* (not thinking about) the path of least resistance.

In line with what we have discussed throughout this chapter, the path of least resistance may or may not be an action path. It may or may not involve any physical action. There have been instances in my life where the path of least resistance was an inner, non-physical path. For example, I often get the feeling that the time is not right for me to act on something. Although there are no physical signs to support my inner knowing, I recognize it as a sign from the Universe. That is when I sit back and do nothing until I receive a different impulse on the inside. I often find that things happen smoothly for me whenever I act according to divine timing.

Sometimes the path of least resistance for a particular situation may be to change the way we feel about that situation on the inside. This is another often-overlooked aspect of our physical manifestations.

Suppose that an individual wants to manifest more financial abundance in their life. At the same time, their consciousness is bogged down by constant worries and negative thoughts about their mounting debt. The path of least resistance for this individual may not be to take any physical actions on the outside, but to simply change the way they *feel* about their debt on the inside. For example, instead of thinking about their debts as insurmountable and blaming themselves for their past choices, they may start by feeling at peace with their financial situation. The path from inner turmoil to inner peace may represent the path of least resistance for them in that situation, which may in turn lead to their final manifestations of abundance.

The path of least resistance does not have to involve doing something big. It can be something seemingly small and insignificant to you. But the fact that you are being called to take that path tells you there is something special about it. This is the path which the Universe *wants* you to take. It is the path which represents the most direct route between where you currently are—and where you want to be.

I have learned over the course of many years never to second-guess the intelligence of the Universe and to always focus single-mindedly on my highest desired outcome in any situation, while leaving the pathways open to the Universe. You don't have to find the path. Let it gently present itself to you. The path will present itself as a gentle beckoning, a calling, where everything feels right along the way. Whatever the path may be, take it when it presents itself. Don't reject it just because it does not seem like the "logical" or right path to take. For example, making peace with your debt may seem like an irresponsible thing to do. Some people are worried that their debts will snowball if they feel "alright" instead of guilty about their financial situation! What kind of twisted logic is that? Being steeped in negative feelings of guilt all day can only lead to more undesired behaviors and manifestations. It was only until I made peace with my situation that I was able to manifest the abundance which I desired. The same applies to any other situation in your life. Seek to remove the negative charge from any situation and then start from a neutral point. Feeling peaceful about the situation does not mean that you condone your past behaviors. Rather, it represents your willingness to be called forth into what comes next, instead of being stuck in the past.

Chapter Eight

Traversing the Chosen Path with Great Delight!

Once you have felt for the path of least resistance, the next step is to allow yourself to traverse it. Traversing the path means taking the next natural step that will move you in that direction. Remember that the path of least resistance feels nothing like strain or struggle. There is no unwillingness or inertia involved. The path of least resistance is a joyful journey in which each step along the way feels right and confirms what you already know on the inside. Your impulse to follow this path is the Universe's way of nudging you toward your greater good.

The actions I feel guided to take may be something as simple as researching a particular topic, clicking on a website link or going to a certain place. At other times, I feel inspired to take bigger actions, like investing in a business or buying a piece of property. Whatever I feel guided to do, I honor my inner nudges because I know what a true intuitive nudge feels like for me on the inside. Over time, I have come to recognize when the Universe is gently guiding me along my path of least resistance and when it is just my fear-based ego-self speaking. While the action I feel inspired to take today may seem insignificant, it may just be what is needed to move me along my highest path. Therefore, never dismiss any inspired action as being "too small" to make a difference. Only the Universe knows the grand scheme of things and how each piece fits.

It wasn't always like this. In the beginning, my intuitive signals were often mixed with messages of fear or urgency conjured by my reasoning mind. Following those false signals brought me on wild journeys I would rather have not been on—but all of those cases eventually taught me precious lessons. In each of those instances and undesired manifestations, I was clarifying my own relationship with the Universe. I was learning to recognize my unique connection to source energy.

This is why the to-do list exercise is so insightful. I know this is probably the tenth time I've advocated that you try this exercise for yourself, but it provides you with a safe way to explore your own connection with the Universe. By learning how to feel for the path of least resistance with regard to your simple, everyday (and largely non-consequential) activities, you strengthen your abilities to recognize when your inner guidance is speaking to you. When you use your inner guidance for the smaller things in life, you sharpen your abilities to use them for the bigger things when the situation calls for it.

Each time you traverse the path of least resistance by taking the next natural step, you solidify and move closer to your desired physical reality. Therefore, the joy is really in the journey! I used to have a difficult time understanding why spiritual teachers would always claim that the real joy lies in the journey (when all I wanted was the stuff I was asking for so badly!), until I realized that there is nothing more fulfilling than seeing one's own creative intentions grow from a mere energetic thought form into a physical creation. Of course, the reverse is also true. There is nothing more distressing than seeing one's negative thoughts materialize as physical reality! This is why it is even more important to learn how to tap into these creative principles in the right way.

Each time you allow yourself to traverse the path of least resistance, you feel the joy associated with taking that step. Since we have already established earlier that *nothing* on the path of least resistance feels like struggle or strain, there is pure unbridled joy in taking each step. These feelings of joy are the ones that will color your life and fill it with joyful moments! No one sums it up better than Abraham-Hicks with the following quote, "A happy life is just a string of happy moments. But most people don't allow the happy moment, because they're so busy trying to get a happy life."

This perspective may seem slightly surprising to you, since the focus of all my books has been on manifesting what you want. But the message here is that the *pathway* to the final manifestation has to be savored and enjoyed as well. If you do not develop an appreciation for the infinite pathways through which your good can come to you and just keep cursing the pathways that are closed off to you, then it will be difficult for physical manifestations to occur in your life. Therefore, manifestations are really about mastering your relationship with the myriad of pathways that are open to you at any one time. In other words, how you *feel* about these pathways will give you an indication as to the speed and efficacy of your physical manifestations.

Before I understood these spiritual principles, I was an extremely judgmental person who was always quick to point out why I couldn't get what I wanted. When a potential pathway was shown to me, for example through books or courses, I was always critical and harsh in passing judgment. Little did I know that I was trying to "figure out" what my manifestation pathway *should* be, through the use of my limited intellect. I was adamant that nothing would work for me; sure enough, nothing worked for many years of my life. I did not realize that by constantly passing judgments and by refusing to entertain an alternative reality, I was in fact closing off a large number of these possible pathways to myself. Pathways which the Universe could have opened for me in an instant!

I see this mistake being made over and over again by so many spiritual "seekers" who are especially harsh on themselves and on others. They are so certain that some of these ideas will never work for them. But how can they be so sure? Perhaps the most succinct summary of the art of manifestations is this: there are infinite pathways through which your good can be delivered to you, but you do not know what these pathways are in advance. You cannot arrive at them through intellectual reasoning and deduction. The only way is to use your inner guidance and intuition to help you along the way.

A common theme of many negative reviews is this, "This is ridiculous and misleading! It does not work!" I always find it amusing that a person who has *not* found a way to make something work criticizes the person who *has* found a way to get results.

While criticism does not change the results obtained by the other person, it keeps us trapped in our own limited thinking and beliefs. This is why I am especially careful nowadays not to fall into this same trap, having fallen into it many times during my early days. When I learn about a new spiritual technique or teaching that seems different to what I am familiar with, my first impulse will often be to dismiss that teaching outright. But wait—what am I really dismissing if the other person has managed to obtain some amazing, replicable results from that practice? My judgments will certainly not change the wonderful experience of the other person. On the contrary, I would be dismissing wonderful opportunities for learning and integrating that knowledge into my own understanding.

I've experienced a delightful expansion of my manifestation abilities since adopting this new playful mindset. For example, I once picked up a book about a spiritual healer who could perform plastic surgery using only his bare hands. Skeptics would be tempted to dismiss his accounts outright, but I kept an open mind. I was not interested in performing the same kind of healing for myself, but was more interested in the beliefs he had which allowed him to perform those miraculous acts. In other words, I was looking for insights into his inner state as he performed those healing miracles. By reading the book between the lines, I was able to pick up on the underlying essence of his miraculous abilities and use them in other areas of my life. Had I insisted on developing the very same healing abilities that he did (the ability to perform plastic surgery using only my hands), I would have severely limited my own possibilities.

Over the years, I realized that every good spiritual teacher provides clear insights into their inner states and beliefs, rather than to just tell you the physical steps involved in the process and then have you follow them. It is not the physical moves but the inner states and inner beliefs that make all of the difference.

What is the inner state in which you should immerse yourself, in order to experience the spontaneous fulfillment of your desires? We have already covered much of them up to this point in the book. First, immerse yourself in the knowledge that an infinite number of manifestation pathways always exist for you, no matter what your situation may be. Second, know that amongst all these pathways, there will be a few which will allow your desires to be delivered to you in the shortest and most direct way possible. These are the paths of least resistance. However, the path of least resistance can never be arrived at through logical deduction or guesswork. You need to follow your heart and use your inner guidance in "feeling for" these pathways of least resistance. Third, allow yourself to joyfully traverse these pathways once you have identified them. This step happens naturally, since one can't ignore these Universal impulses forever.

There is no need to deliberately look out for these pathways as you go about your daily life. Instead, your entire focus should be on enjoying each moment of life and taking the path of least resistance in each moment. Always ask yourself: "What is the path of least resistance that I can take in this moment?" Then relax, and let the answer reveal itself to you in terms of an inner feeling. You'll find that your higher self always knows the answer to this question, and will always be able to guide you intuitively to your path of least resistance in each moment.

It is important to remain open to all possibilities. Sometimes, you may find that the path of least resistance is to finally do a piece of work which you have been putting off for the longest time. While your logical mind wishes to procrastinate further, you may receive a clear intuitive nudge that now is the right time for the task. And so you pick up the phone and make the necessary phone calls. I often find that tasks I've been putting off for the longest time are completed with astonishing ease as I am connected to the right people or with the right resources. The Universe truly has its own way of making things happen.

On other occasions, you may perceive a pressing need to complete an urgent task, but may instead feel that the path of least resistance is to do nothing at all! This is perhaps the most difficult of impulses to follow since ignoring a tight deadline seems irresponsible by societal standards. But once you strengthen your own unique connection to the Universe and know how the path of least resistance feels, you will find that taking this path pays off every single time. Whenever I heed the Universe's advice to do nothing despite an urgent deadline around the corner, two things usually happen: the situation may resolve itself without the need for my active intervention, or an even better solution may present itself along the way as I am engaged in another activity.

By keeping my focus on my desired outcome and not worrying about how I will get there, I allow the Universe, in all of its infinite intelligence, to deliver my desired outcome to me through the shortest possible pathways.

CHAPTER NINE

LETTING YOUR GOOD BE THERE...WHEN YOU GET THERE!

Abraham-Hicks have long spoken about the importance of pre-paving and how it relates to the manifestation process. This is also an aspect of manifestation which I have not touched upon in great detail in my previous books, however the theme of our current discussion offers a wonderful opportunity to do so. Understanding the role of pre-paving and how it relates to your final manifestations can make a huge difference to the speed and timing of the fulfillment of your desires.

To the layperson, the act of pre-paving is nothing more than becoming mentally prepared for our final manifestations. One may assume that when Abraham-Hicks speak about the importance of pre-paving for our desired manifestations, it simply means to think and visualize more about what we want with a certain sense of positive expectancy. However, the significance of pre-paving goes further and deeper than that.

Pre-paving is not a repetitive act of mental preparation where you repeatedly think about what you want in order to make things happen faster. Instead, pre-paving is the act of planting something in your future reality so solidly, that what you desire **will be there in physical form when you get there**.

Once you have effectively pre-paved, you no longer worry about when or whether your manifestations will happen for you. You just know that anytime you hold a pure intention for something on the inside, it becomes automatically activated somewhere in your future reality. As you traverse the path of least resistance and step into that future reality, what you have asked for previously is right there waiting for you. You literally step right into what you have pre-paved. There is nothing else you have to do to make things happen. This is the immense power that comes from proper pre-paving.

But how do we effectively pre-pave for our future? How do we let our good be there—when we get there? This is where everything we have discussed in this book finally comes together. We are already pre-paving our future whether we like it or not. We are, in this very moment, choosing what goes into our future experiences based on our thoughts, preferences and feelings in the current moment. For most people, their habits of thought will ensure that their future looks very much like their past and present, which also means little or no improvement in their current conditions. They are being propelled forward by their habitual patterns of thought, and life takes on a foreseeable trajectory for them. However, as a conscious student of these Universal principles, *you* know better. You know that anytime you hold an intention for an alternate reality, that reality already exists *somewhere out there* in the future. You also know that there are infinite pathways standing between your current self and that desired future outcome, and that taking any one of these pathways can easily bring you to straight to that desired outcome.

Most people expect a certain positive outcome and then are quick to notice all the obstacles that stand in their way. They are quick to explain why various pathways are closed off to them because of certain inherent limitations. But little do they know that an *infinite* number of pathways exist even for them! If they would just be willing to ponder the truth—that an infinite number of options are available for their taking in every moment—and be led to take those pathways...then whatever they are asking for *will happen* for them, extremely quick.

Quite simply, we start the pre-paving process by holding our highest desired outcomes in mind and momentarily forgetting about the possible pathways to get there. Since there is an infinite number of pathways, our good **has** to happen every time we ask. There are unlimited ways to make things happen; this is Universal Law. This is why spiritual teachers often teach that the Universe always answers in the moment that we ask, and that we are always given what we ask for, without exception.

Each time we affirm our highest desired outcomes, we solidify future reality. Our pure intentions are more than just thoughts and mental activities on the inside. Our intentions are energetic thought forms that have the ability to influence other thought forms, and hence have the ability to shape the energetic fields (realities) around us.

Once you have asked for something, the next step is to sit back and relax, knowing that it is already somewhere out there in your probable future. Now all that is left to do—is to step into that future! You step into that future by choosing, on a moment-to-moment basis, the paths of least resistance that present themselves for you. If you'll only take the next natural step that feels right for you, followed by the next natural step after that, then life becomes easy and effortless. It is only when you demand to see the whole staircase that life becomes a struggle and is filled with great uncertainties. Don't demand to see the whole staircase. Instead, just *know* that the path is there, and that you are being led to take the next step in divine timing.

The whole staircase (or path) cannot possibly be shown to you all at once because the path is open to change in every moment. Think about it like a flowing river. One may be able to chart an imagined path for how water should flow between two points, but that path is always subject to change. If a new channel of lesser resistance appears, the water effortlessly changes its course and takes that new path. If an earlier path turns out to be blocked, the water does not stagnate at that spot demanding that the path be unblocked. Instead, the water automatically seeks out a new path of least resistance and masterfully works around any obstacles as they arise. As far as the flowing water is concerned, there are no limitations. Perhaps this is why the Taoist masters like Lao Tzu have developed such a special affinity for water and frequently use it in their analogies: "Water is the softest thing, yet it can penetrate mountains and earth."

In the same vein, the Universe is simultaneously responding to the needs and desires of billions of organisms, each of them with their own preferences and intentions. From its perspective, the Universe plays the role of a master coordinator, matching up different individuals with other people, places and circumstances. The Universe does so with a sense of precision and ease that is unimaginable from our limited human perspectives. Thankfully, we don't have to fill the Universe's shoes. We don't even have to know the mechanics of how the Universe does its job. All we need to develop is an appreciation for these Universal principles and learn how to live in accordance with them.

When I ask for something in my life today, I no longer worry about when it will appear in my reality. Neither do I demand that it shows up immediately in my life. Instead, I know that things I asked for *have to* happen, so why worry about the timing, making myself unhappy in the meantime? I just ask with the purest of intentions, knowing that there are infinite pathways to make things happen, and then let it go completely. I take great joy in planting these delightful manifestations in my future reality, which often surprise me when I walk right into them. I do this so frequently now that I often forget what I have asked for in the past. It is only with the physical manifestation that I am reminded of the seed which I planted not too long before.

Perhaps it is time that you adopt a similar childlike attitude toward your manifestations. Forget whatever you have asked for and ask without any expectations of the past, present or future. Ask with the sure knowledge that things will happen to you, since there are infinite manifestation pathways leading to your good. When you develop such a relationship with your inner self, then the manifestation process becomes fun and easy. Manifestations no longer center upon hit rates or keeping score. I am often amused when individuals share their success rates when using a particular manifestation technique in the hopes of discovering a technique with a higher "hit rate." They say things like, "Using technique A, I have about a 50% success rate as compared to technique B, which gives me a 70% success rate."

Why limit yourself in this way? Your success rate is *already* one hundred percent because the Universe answers one hundred percent of the time! You are already getting what you ask for one hundred percent of the time, it's just that you have not traversed some of the paths to those future probable realities yet! So stop believing in the illusion by claiming that things only happen for you half of the time. As a creator at the core of your being, you deserve to have what you ask for one hundred percent of the time, no matter what it is you may be asking for.

The question then becomes: is your inner state conducive to these physical manifestations one hundred percent of the time? Or are you constantly steeped in negative feelings of worry, anger, jealously, guilt or fear? Are you acting—and more important, feeling—in accordance with how a one-hundred-percent manifestor *should* act and feel?

It is time to claim your one hundred percent success rate for yourself! The best way is to quit thinking in terms of statistics and hit rates. A more resourceful way to think about your manifestations will be this: "All of my intentions are acted upon by the Universe. Some have become manifest in my current reality, while others are still in the process of becoming. I treat all of my intentions the same, whether those that are manifest or are not-yet-manifest."

Doesn't this shift make you feel much better instantly? Instead of blaming yourself or feeling resentful about all of the things that have not yet come into your life, develop an appreciation for the things that have happened so far and for the things that are in the process of becoming. This is not just a way to make ourselves feel better. You must know that each time you ask, the Universe answers and already knows all possible pathways. Therefore, it is more preposterous to believe that you are ever denied from having something than to believe that you can have everything! Know that your inten-tions are *always* coming into form for you and live in accordance with that knowledge by letting the Universe show you the path of least resistance out of all the paths that are possible.

And don't worry if you miss a particular path or opportunity. There is never just one pathway toward your good. There is always another path, and another path, and another path that awaits you after that. The Universe will keep nudging you toward the appropriate path in any situation until you take heed!

I started my conscious spiritual journey more than ten years ago. The first few years of my journey were filled with lack, limitation and suffering because I wasn't aware of the infinite pathways that were available to me. I kept insisting on doing things my own way and traversing the same few pathways which I logically figured out. When there were no visible options in sight, I became negative, resentful and depressed. My stubborn insistence on figuring out a way for myself led to many "missed" opportunities. But still infinite options continued to be available to me the whole time. The moment I opened my eyes to the true nature of our wonderful Universe and saw how I had been working against myself all this while, everything changed. That was when I found my desired good—and my good found me. The best part in all of this? My manifestations became as effortless as merely *thinking* about them. All the hard work has been taken out of the equation.

Now that you understand the principle of infinite manifestation pathways, what should you do next? Perhaps the more appropriate question should be, what should you *not* do next? Whatever the answer may be, I can't answer it for you. The answer is always right there within yourself. Feel for it and then allow yourself to be carried away by the joy in every moment of life. If you'll just do so for the rest of your life, focusing on one now-moment after another, then you'll not only have a long string of happy moments, but also several handfuls of absolutely wondrous manifestations. And even *that* will be a gross understatement!

ABOUT THE AUTHOR

Richard Dotts is a modern-day spiritual explorer. An avid student of ancient and modern spiritual practices, Richard shares how to apply these timeless principles in our daily lives. For more than a decade, he has experimented with these techniques himself, studying why they work and separating the science from the superstition. In the process, he has created successful careers as an entrepreneur, business owner, author and teacher.

Leading a spiritual life does not mean walking away from your current life and giving up everything you have. The core of his teachings is that you can lead a spiritual and magical life starting right now, from where you are, in whatever field you are in.

You can make a unique contribution to the world, because you are blessed with the abilities of a true creator. By learning how to shape the energy around you, your life can change in an instant, if you allow it to!

Richard is the author of more than 20 Amazon bestsellers on the science of manifestation and reality creation.

An Introduction to the Manifestations Approach of Richard Dotts

Even after writing more than 20 Amazon bestsellers on the subject of creative manifestations and leading a fulfilling life, Richard Dotts considers himself to be more of an adventurous spiritual explorer than a spiritual teacher or "master", as some of his readers have called him by.

"When you apply these spiritual principles in your own life, you will realize that everyone is a master, with no exceptions. Everyone has the power to design and create his own life on his own terms," says Richard.

"Therefore, there is no need to give up your power by going through an intermediary or any spiritual medium. Each time you buy into the belief that your good can only come through a certain teacher or a certain channel…you give up the precious opportunity to realize your own good. My best teachers were those who helped me recognize the innate power within myself, and kept the faith for me even when I could not see this spiritual truth for myself."

Due to his over-questioning and skeptical nature (unaided by the education which he received over the years), Richard struggled with the application of these spiritual principles in his early years.

After reading thousands of books on related subjects and learning about hundreds of different spiritual traditions with little success, Richard realized there was still one place left unexplored.

It was a place that he was the most afraid to look at: **his inner state.**

Richard realized that while he had been applying these Universal principles and techniques dutifully on the outside, his inner state remained tumultuous the whole time. Despite being well-versed in these spiritual principles, he was constantly plagued with negative feelings of worry, fear, disappointment, blame, resentment and guilt on the inside during his waking hours. These negative feelings and thoughts drained him of much of his energy and well-being.

It occurred to him that unless he was free from these negative feelings and habitual patterns of thought, any outer techniques he tried would not work. That was when he achieved his first spiritual breakthrough and saw improvements in his outer reality.

Taking A Light Touch

The crux of Richard's teachings is that one has to do the inner work first by tending to our own inner states. No one else, not even a powerful spiritual master, can do this for us. Once we have restored our inner state to a place of *zero*, a place of profound calmness and peace…that is when miracles can happen. Any subsequent intention that is held with <u>a light touch</u> in our inner consciousness quickly becomes manifest in our outer reality.

Through his books and teachings, Richard continually emphasizes the importance of taking a light touch. This means adopting a carefree, playful and detached attitude when working with these Universal Laws.

"Whenever we become forceful or desperate in asking for what we want, we invariably delay or withhold our own good. This is because we start to feel even more negative feelings of desperation and worry, which cloud our inner states further and prevent us from receiving what we truly want."

To share these realizations with others, Richard has written a series of books on various aspects of these manifestation principles and Universal Laws. Each of his books touches on a different piece of the manifestation puzzle that he has struggled with in the past.

For example, there are certain books that guide readers through the letting-go of negative feelings and the dropping of negative beliefs. There are books that talk about how to deal with self-doubt and a lack of faith in the application of these spiritual principles. Yet other books offer specific techniques for holding focused intentions in our inner consciousness. A couple of books deal with advanced topics such as nonverbal protocols for the manifestation process.

Richard's main goal is to break down the mysterious and vast subject of spiritual manifestations into easy to understand pieces for the modern reader. While he did not invent these Universal Laws and is certainly not the first to write about them, Richard's insights are valuable in showing readers how to easily apply these spiritual principles despite leading modern and hectic lifestyles. Thus, a busy mother of three or the CEO of a large corporation can just as easily access these timeless spiritual truths through Richard's works, as an ancient ascetic who lived quietly by himself.

It is Richard's intention to show readers that miracles are still possible in our modern world. When you experience the transformational power of these teachings for yourself, you stop seeing them as unexpected miracles and start seeing them as part of your everyday reality.

Do I have to read every book in order to create my own manifestation miracles?

Because Richard is unbounded by any spiritual or religious tradition, his work is continuously evolving based on a fine-tuning of his own personal experiences. He does, however, draw his inspiration from a broad range of teachings. Richard writes for the primary purpose of sharing his own realizations and not for any commercial interest, which is why he has shied away from the publicity that typically comes with being a bestselling author.

All of his books have achieved Amazon bestseller status with no marketing efforts or publicity, a testament to the effectiveness of his methods. An affiliation with a publishing house could mean a pressure to write books on certain popular subjects, or a need to censor the more esoteric and non-traditional aspects of his writing. Therefore, Richard has taken great steps to ensure his freedom as a writer. It is this freedom that keeps him prolific.

One of Richard's aims is to help readers apply these principles in their lives with minimal struggle or strain, which is why he has offered in-depth guidance on many related subjects. Richard himself has maintained that there is no need to read each and every single one of his books. Instead, one should just narrow in to the particular aspects that they are struggling with.

As he explains in his own words, "You can read just one book and completely change your life on the basis of that book if you internalized its teachings. You can do this not only with my books, but also with the books of any other author."

"For me, the journey took a little longer. One book could not do it for me. I struggled to overcome years of negative programming and critical self-talk, so much so that reading thousands of books did not help me as well. But after I reached that critical tipping point, when I finally 'got it', then I started to get everything. The first book, the tenth book, the hundredth book I read all started to make sense. I could pick up any book I read in the past and intuitively understand the spiritual essence of what the author was saying. But till I reached that point of understand within myself, I could not do so."

Therefore, one only needs to read as many books as necessary to achieve a true understanding on the inside. Beyond that, any reading is for one's personal enjoyment and for a fine-tuning of the process.

Which book should I start with?

There is no prescribed reading order. Start with the book that most appeals to you or the one that you feel most inspired to read. Each Richard Dotts book is self-contained and is written such that the reader can instantly benefit from the teachings within, no matter which stage of life they are at. If any prerequisite or background knowledge is needed, Richard will suggest additional resources within the text.

OTHER BOOKS
BY RICHARD DOTTS

Many of these titles are progressively offered in various formats (both in hard copy and eBook formats). Our intention is to eventually make all these titles available in hard copy format.

- **Banned Manifestation Secrets**
  It all starts here! In this book, Richard lays out the fundamental principles of spiritual manifestations and explains common misconceptions about the "Law of Attraction." This is also the book where Richard first talks about the importance of one's inner state in creating outer manifestations.
- **Come and Sit With Me (Book 1): How to Desire Nothing and Manifest Everything**
  If you had one afternoon with Richard Dotts, what questions would you ask him about manifesting your desires and the creative process? In Come and Sit With Me, Richard candidly answers some of the most pressing questions that have been asked by his readers. Written in a

free-flowing and conversational format, Richard addresses some of the most relevant issues related to manifestations and the application of these spiritual principles in our daily lives. Rather than shying away from tough questions about the manifestation process, Richard dives into them head-on and shows the readers practical ways in which they can use to avoid common manifestation pitfalls.

- **The Magic Feeling Which Creates Instant Manifestations**
  Is there really a "magic feeling", an inner state of mind that results in almost instant manifestations? Can someone live in a perpetual state of grace, and have good things and all your deepest desires come true spontaneously without any "effort" on your part? In this book, Richard talks about why the most effective part of visualizations lies in the *feelings*...and how to get in touch with this magic feeling.

- **Playing In Time And Space: The Miracle of Inspired Manifestations**
  In Playing In Time And Space, Richard Dotts shares the secrets to creating our own physical reality from our current human perspectives. Instead of seeing the physical laws of space and time as restricting us, Richard shares how anyone can transcend these perceived limitations of space and time by changing their thinking, and manifest right from where they are.

- **Allowing Divine Intervention**

  Everyone talks about wanting to live a life of magic and miracles, but what does a miracle really look like? Do miracles only happen to certain spiritual people, or at certain points in our lives (for example, at our most desperate)? Is it possible to lead an everyday life filled with magic, miracles and joy?

  In Allowing Divine Intervention, Richard explains how miracles and divine interventions are not reserved for the select few, but can instead be experienced by anyone willing to change their current perceptions of reality.

- **It is Done! The Final Step To Instant Manifestations**

  The first time Richard Dotts learnt about the significance of the word "Amen" frequently used in prayers…goosebumps welled up all over his body and everything clicked in place for him. Suddenly, everything he had learnt up to that point about manifestations made complete sense.

  In It Is Done!, Richard Dotts explores the hidden significance behind these three simple words in the English language. Three words, when strung together and used in the right fashion, holds the keys to amazingly accurate and speedy manifestations.

- **Banned Money Secrets**

  In Banned Money Secrets of the Hidden Rich, Richard explains how there is a group of individuals in our midst, coming from almost every walk of life, who have developed a special relationship with money. These are the individuals for whom money seems to flow easily at will, which has allowed them to live exceedingly creative and fulfilled lives unlimited by money. More surprisingly, Richard discovered that there is not a single common characteristic that unites the "hidden rich" except for their unique ability to focus intently on their desires to the exclusion of everything else. Some of the "hidden rich" are the most successful multi-millionaires and billionaires of our time, making immense contributions in almost every field.

Richard teaches using his own life examples that the only true, lasting source of abundance comes from behaving like one of the hidden rich, and from developing an extremely conducive inner state that allows financial abundance to easily flow into your life.

- **The 95-5 Code: for Activating the Law of Attraction**
  Most books and courses on the Law of Attraction teach various outer-directed techniques one can use to manifest their desires. All is well and good, but an important question remains unanswered: What do you do during the remainder of your time when you are not actively using these manifestation techniques? How do you live? What do you do with the 95% of your day, the majority of your waking hours when you are not actively asking for what you want? Is the

"rest of your day" important to the manifestation process?

It turns out that what you do during the 95% of your time, the time NOT spent visualizing or affirming, makes all of the difference.

In The 95-5 Code for activating the Law of Attraction, Richard Dotts explains why the way you act (and feel) during the majority of your waking hours makes all the difference to your manifestation end results.

- **Inner Confirmation for Outer Manifestations**

How do you know if things are on their way after you have asked for them?

What should you do after using a particular manifestation technique?

What does evidence of your impending manifestations feel like?

You may not have seen yourself as a particularly spiritual or intuitive person, much less an energy reader...but join Richard Dotts as he explains in Inner Confirmation for Outer Manifestations how everyone can easily perceive the energy fields around them.

- **Mastering the Manifestation Paradox**

The Manifestation Paradox is an inner riddle that quickly becomes apparent to anyone who has been exposed to modern day Law of Attraction and manifestation teachings. It is an inner state that seems to be contradictory to the person practicing it, yet one that is associated with inevitably fast physical manifestations—that of *wanting* something and yet at the same time *not wanting* it.

Richard Dotts explains why the speed and timing of our manifestations depends largely on our mastery of the Manifestation Paradox. Through achieving a deeper understanding of this paradox, we can consciously and deliberately move all our desires (even those we have been struggling with) to a "sweet spot" where physical manifestations *have to occur* very quickly for us instead of having our manifestations happen "by default."

- **Today I Am Free: Manifesting Through Deep Inner Changes**
  In Today I Am Free, Richard Dotts returns with yet another illuminating discussion of these timeless Universal Laws and spiritual manifestation principles. While his previous works focused on letting go of the worry and fear feelings that prevent our manifestations from happening in our lives, Today I Am Free focuses on a seldom discussed aspect of our lives that can affect our manifestations in a big way: namely our interaction with others and the judgments, opinions and perceptions that other people may hold of us. Richard Dotts shows readers simple ways in which they can overcome their constant feelings of fear and self-consciousness to be truly free.

- **Dollars Flow To Me Easily**

  Is it possible to read and relax your way into financial abundance? Can dollars flow to you even if you just sat quietly in your favorite armchair and did "nothing"? Is abundance and prosperity really our natural birthright, as claimed by so many spiritual masters and authors throughout the ages?

  Dollars Flow To Me Easily takes an alternative approach to answering these questions. Instead of guiding the reader through a series of exercises to "feel as if" they are already rich, Richard draws on the power of words and our highest intentions to dissolve negative feelings and misconceptions that block us from manifesting greater financial abundance in our lives.

- **Light Touch Manifestations: How To Shape The Energy Field To Attract What You Want**

  Richard covers the entire manifestation sequence in detail, showing exactly how our beliefs and innermost thoughts can lead to concrete, outer manifestations. As part of his approach of taking a light touch, Richard shows readers how to handle each component of the manifestation sequence and tweak it to produce fast, effective manifestations in our daily lives.

- **Infinite Manifestations: The Power of Stopping at Nothing**

  In Infinite Manifestations, Richard shares a practical, step-by-step method for erasing the unconscious memories and blocks that hold our manifestations back. The Infinite Release technique, "revealed" to Richard by the Universe, is a quick and easy way to let go of any unconscious memories, blocks and resistances that may prevent our highest good from coming to us. When we invoke the Infinite Release process, we are no longer doing it alone. Instead, we step out of the way, letting go and letting God. We let Universal Intelligence decide how our inner resistances and blocks should be dissolved. All we need to do is to intend that we are clear from these blocks that hold us back. Once the Infinite Release process is invoked, it is done!

- **Let The Universe Lead You!**
  Imagine what your life would be like if you could simply hold an intention for something…and then be led clearly and precisely, every single time, to the fulfilment of your deepest desires. No more wondering about whether you are on the "right" path or making the "right" moves. No more second-guessing yourself or acting out of desperation—You simply set an intention and allow the Universe to lead you to it effortlessly!

- **Manifestation Pathways: Letting Your Good Be There…When You Get There!**
  Imagine having a desire for something and then immediately intuiting (knowing) what the path of least resistance should be for that desire. When you allow the Universe to lead you in this manner and unfold the manifestation pathway

of least resistance to you, then life becomes as effortless as knowing what you want, planting it in your future reality and letting your good be there when you get there...every single time! This book shows you the practical techniques to make it happen in your life.

- **And more...**

Made in the USA
Middletown, DE
31 January 2023